Nonnie's Kitchen

Fun & Food in the Kitchen

with Kids

By Tonya Greenfield

M2MPartners
publishing

scottsdale   los angeles   london

Published by M2M Partners Publishing
7825 E. Redfield Road, Suite 101
Scottsdale, Arizona 85260-6977
(800) 658-8790

ISBN: 0-9768884-0-8

This book is available for bulk purchases as
premiums or special editions, including
personalized covers. For more information,
contact the publisher at:
orders@nonnieskitchen.com

Printed in the United States.

10 9 8 7 6 5 4 3 2 1

Dedication

As a small child, I learned so much from the sweetest, most patient person in the world . . . my grandmother, my Nonnie. There was never a "no" in her vocabulary . . . ever. When I would make mistakes, she always encouraged me to go forward with my creativity and love of cooking, which began at the age of 4. Maybe not fashionable when I was young, but cooking has always held a special place in my life.

We started out measuring and stirring ingredients together. Grammy (as I liked to call her) loved for me to set the table and, of course, I would volunteer to help clean up the dirty dishes. My fondest memories were when we would spend an afternoon making and decorating spritz cookies for Christmas.

I dedicate this book to all of the Grandmothers, Nonnies and Grammies from all corners of the world that provide a kind heart, a patient demeanor and a spoon of love.

AVO   bunica   grandmother   avia

Babcia   Nonna   grandmére

Bubbie   BaBa   abuela

mormor

Table of Contents

✂ = craft

89 Holidays

How to use Nonnie's Cookbook...

So you want to cook, now?

This is a cookbook for children to use with a grownup or on their own. I have specially created many recipes to introduce you to the world of cooking. I hope that you will be patient, eager to learn and most of all – have a great time in the kitchen.

Throughout this book you will be introduced to many cooking methods, rules of thumb and to some of my fun ideas. I know that you will want to do many of these recipes alone . . . and some, you may . . . but I ask that you get permission from a grownup and that you are supervised at all times. Safety in the kitchen will ensure your success.

A NOTE: Scattered throughout the book, you will notice the green words. These are cooking terms that you may look up in the Glossary at the back of the book. I know that this will be helpful in completing your recipes and will introduce you to the world of cooking.

Cooking Clean & Careful

Important:

There's more to cooking than meets the eye. Planning, buying, storing, preparing and cooking are all important parts of cooking healthy when it comes to good eating. Preparation of food starts with clean hands, clean counter tops, clean utensils and fresh food.

Remember to:

- Clean you hands frequently.
- Store refrigerated foods at 41 degrees Fahrenheit or lower.
- Keep food covered when in the refrigerator.
- Always check the "use by" dates on the packaging.
- Discard out-of-date food products.
- Wash all foods that need cleaning.
- Make sure the food is cooked thoroughly and only reheat once.
- Remember to be very careful.
- Ask a grownup before you use sharp objects like knives.
- Always have a grownup with you in the kitchen when using the stovetop, oven or any other electric appliances.
- Slice, dice and chop on a cutting board with grownup's supervision.
- Turn pan handles to the back of the range to avoid spills and accidents.
- Never put your face near a stovetop burner for any reason.
- Read your recipe and follow the directions carefully.
- Most important, have fun learning your way around the kitchen.

Cooking Methods

There are many ways to cook. Understanding them will be necessary to complete many of my recipes in this book. These are the methods that you should know . . .

Baking

Baking is the term for cooking food in the oven by dry heat. It is a process for preparing baked goods, such as cookies and pies. Bake foods uncovered for dry crisp surfaces (bread, cakes, cookies or chicken) or cover food with aluminum foil or a lid for moistness.

Boiling

Food is cooked in a liquid, such as water, soup stock or milk to a high temperature. Lots of bubbles will appear when it has successfully boiled and steam rises from the cooking pot.

Broiling

To cook food directly under a heat source.

Deep Frying

To submerge and cook food in very hot oil until crisp on the outside. This method must be supervised by a grownup.

Frying

This is a process of cooking food in hot butter or oil, usually until a crisp brown crust forms. This method is usually cooked in a skillet on the stove-top.

Griddling

To griddle refers to cooking on a rigid pan like a waffle iron, to cook healthy and without any fats. Great for making food such as, waffles, crepes or panini.

Grilling

To grill is to cook over an open flame on a barbeque or camp fire. This is perhaps the oldest method of cooking.

Microwaving

A fast cooking oven, which is heated through electric microwaves. A lot of foods today can be prepared in a microwave, allowing for shorter cooking times. Heats thoroughly, but usually doesn't brown.

Toasting

To heat and brown on all sides, by placing in a toaster or an oven.

> " Cooking is so much fun and knowing these methods, will make it all the more eventful. Now I think you are ready to prepare everything in this book! "

Setting the Table

There are many versions of table settings. But the traditional, informal setting of the table is a good place to start. When setting the table, place silverware in the order of use. The fork and napkin are always on the left side of the plate and the knife and spoon go on the right. Drinking glasses go above the knife and spoon.

IDEA On holidays and special occasions, spread butcher paper over the tablecloth and set colored crayons at each place setting. It is loads of fun to doodle while waiting for the next course. Or better yet, set your table with all different plates and different colored napkins tied with ribbon or string from which a name tag hangs. Or for more fun, attach a trinket belonging to each guest. Let them guess where they should be seated.

ANOTHER IDEA Create placemats, using construction paper, crayons, lace, leaves or photographs. Draw your favorite flowers. Be original. Try making a special occasion placemat for your family, so they will have a keepsake of their own.

> " My grandchildren always make placemats for my birthday dinner. What a delightful keepsake that I can share with them as they grow older. Wonderful memories are what it is all about. "

Good Morning!

Saturday morning is a special time to get creative with breakfast. My five Grandchildren love to spend the night at Nonnie's. They especially look forward to the morning, when we all prepare breakfast. I always make sure each child has a job putting the most important meal of the day together. We always start with juice, which is usually gone before the first plate hits the table. Of course, there is always fresh fruit, sausage and bacon to go along with breakfast.

Oh, and when it is time to clean up, everyone scatters

One Egg in a Hole

serves 4

Nonnie's Kitchen
INGREDIENTS

- 4 Bread Slices
- 8 Tablespoons Butter
- 4 Eggs
- 1 Cup Cooked Bacon Bits

microwave

Cut a hole in the center of each slice of your favorite bread. You can use a biscuit cutter if you like to make a perfect circle. Butter the bread generously on both sides with butter

fry

Melt 3 tablespoon of butter in a skillet. Place as many slices as you can in a skillet. You may have to do 2 slices at a time. Brown the buttered bread slices on both sides. Crack an egg and drop it into the center of each of the browned bread slices. Cover with a lid. Cook until the white of the egg is fully cooked, longer if you like harder eggs. Remove from the pan with a spatula.

serve

Sprinkle your egg with cooked bacon bits and serve.

> 66 The only problem is whether to eat the toast first or the egg. No matter what, it will taste great. 99

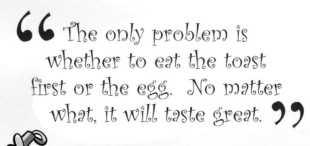

Drop Kick Biscuits

Nonnie's Kitchen

INGREDIENTS

2 Cups Sifted Flour
3 Teaspoons Baking
  Powder
1 Teaspoon Salt
1/3 Cup Butter or Crisco®
3/4 Cup Whole Milk

prepare

Heat the oven to 450 degrees. Spray a cookie sheet with vegetable spray so the biscuits won't stick. Mix together the flour, baking powder and salt. **Cut in** the shortening into the dry mixture. With a fork, stir in the milk. Do not stir for very long, just until all ingredients are pretty well together and sticky. Flour your hands and pick up the dough mixture with a spoon and drop onto the cookie sheet, leaving about 2 inches between biscuits. Use your floured hands to remove the biscuit dough from the spoon.

bake

Bake for 10 to 12 minutes or until lightly brown on top.

serve

Serve with jam & jelly, honey, butter or your favorite toppings. Or make a breakfast sandwich with sausage, egg and cheese.

Cin-Mon Toast

Nonnie's Kitchen

INGREDIENTS

3/4 Cup Sugar
4 Teaspoons Cinnamon
6 (1/2 inch thick) Slices
   Home Style or
   Homemade Bread
1 Stick Butter, Melted

prepare

Heat oven to 375 degrees.
Remove the crust from the bread
and cut each slice into thirds, length-wise. In a
wide shallow bowl, mix together the cinnamon and sugar. Take
each piece of bread and dip it in the melted butter, turning
quickly, coating both sides and letting the excess drip off.
Then quickly dip in the cinnamon sugar mixture, coating the
bread on both sides. Place the coated bread on a cookie sheet
that has been sprayed with vegetable spray.

bake

Bake for 10 minutes. Turn the
toast over with a fork and bake
10 minutes more.

serve

Serve while the toast is still
warm. You can serve with orange
juice or fruit.

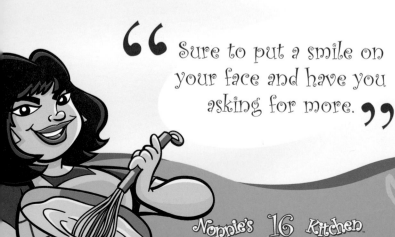

" Sure to put a smile on
your face and have you
asking for more. "

Charlie Brown Breakfast

Nonnie's Kitchen
INGREDIENTS

1 to 2 Lb. Bag Hash Brown Potatoes
1-1/2 Lbs. Ground Sausage
1/2 Onion, Finely Chopped
1 Cup Shredded Cheddar Cheese
5 Eggs
1 (13 oz.) Can Evaporated Milk
1/4 Teaspoon Black Pepper

prepare

Heat the oven to 400 degrees. Grease a 9x13-inch baking dish with vegetable spray. Firmly press uncooked potatoes in the bottom and up the sides of the dish.

bake

Bake the potatoes in the oven for 20 minutes.

fry

In a skillet, brown the sausage and chopped onion until thoroughly cooked. Drain.

prepare

Spread the sausage and onion over the potato crust. Beat the eggs with a whisk, slowly adding the evaporated milk and pepper. Pour the egg mixture over the sausage. Sprinkle the cheddar cheese over the top.

bake

Bake for 20 to 25 minutes or until golden brown.

serve

Serve with fresh fruit, toast, a beverage and . . . your good to go.

Mixed Up Eggs

Nonnie's Kitchen
INGREDIENTS

4 Eggs
1/2 Teaspoon Vanilla
2 Tablespoons Milk
2 Teaspoons Butter
Dash of Onion Salt

prepare

Break eggs into a bowl. **Beat** the eggs with a fork or a small whisk. Add the vanilla and onion salt and whisk again until light and fluffy.

fry

Heat a small skillet with butter. When the butter is melted, move the pan around until butter coats the bottom of the skillet. With the help of a grownup, pour the eggs into the skillet and scramble eggs around gently until eggs are cooked but still moist and shiny.

serve

Serve on a fun or pretty plate with a slice of Cin-Mon Toast (see recipe on page 16) and a piece of fruit. A perfect, quick and delicious breakfast.

Little People Breakfast Cakes

prepare

Separate three eggs, allowing the white of the egg to run into one bowl, and the yolk to run into another. Using a fork or whisk, beat the yolks until frothy. Add the milk, water, matzo meal, salt and sugar. Beat together. Beat the egg whites with a hand mixer on high until the whites look like whipped cream. Fold into the matzo mixture.

Nonnie's Kitchen
INGREDIENTS

3 Extra Large Eggs
1 Stick Butter
1/2 Cup Water
1 Cup Matzo Meal
1/2 Cup Milk
1/2 Teaspoon Salt
1/2 Teaspoon Sugar

fry

In a large skillet, add half of a stick of butter and wait until it sizzles. Drop one tablespoon of batter per pancake into the pan. Six pancakes should fit in a large skillet at one time. The mixture will be very thin, but sets up quickly. Flip over after 30 seconds or until brown. Remove the first batch from the pan and continue dropping mixture by tablespoons full until all the batter is gone. Add butter as needed.

serve

Some like jelly on top, others use syrup and even sour cream. Serve it your way.

Flying Saucer Pancake

Nonnie's Kitchen
INGREDIENTS

6 Extra Large Eggs
1 Cup Flour
1/4 Teaspoon Salt
2 Tablespoons Sugar
1 Cup Milk
3 Tablespoons Butter
(not margarine)
1/4 Cup Powdered Sugar
1/2 Lemon

prepare

Heat oven to 400 degrees. Use a round 10-inch cake pan or any round pan with high sides that can be put in the oven. Spray the pan with vegetable spray. Place the butter in the pan and put the pan in the oven until the butter melts. Carefully take the pan from the oven and swirl the melted butter around until the pan is coated with the butter. In a mixing bowl, whisk the eggs until frothy. Slowly add the flour, sugar, salt and milk. Mix only until all ingredients are blended. A few lumps in the mixture are okay. Pour the batter into the prepared pan.

" This dish is perfect for comapny because it's pretty as a picture and as yummy as it gets. "

bake

Bake for 15 minutes. After 15 minutes, turn down the heat to 325 degrees for 30 additional minutes. It is important that you don't open the oven because it will cause the pancake to fall or not rise properly. When the pancake is done it will be lightly brown on top. Remove the tall, souffle-like pancake from the oven and squeeze lemon juice all over the pancake and dust with powdered sugar.

serve

Remove the pancake from the pan and place on a serving platter. Cut into 6 pieces. Set pancake with toppings on a buffet counter. Let everyone fix their own pancake.

IDEA While the pancake is cooking, gather together choices for toppings. My family likes mixed berries, sour cream and raspberry preserves all together or separately.

Mother's Potatoeggs

Nonnie's Kitchen

INGREDIENTS

3 Large White Baking potatoes
6 Extra Large Eggs
1/2 Cup Cooking Oil
2 Tablespoons Butter

prepare

Peel and cut the potatoes in 1/8-inch slices.
Spray a 10-inch skillet with vegetable spray.

fry

Begin heating the frying pan, adding the oil slowly. Once the oil is in the skillet and hot, put in the potatoes. Cook on medium heat until the potatoes are well browned. Add the Butter to the skillet. In a separate bowl, mix the eggs well with a fork. Pour the eggs over the potatoes. Scramble the potatoes and eggs around until the eggs coat the potatoes and the eggs look well done.

serve

Remove the Potatoeggs from the frying pan and serve in bowls. Serve with a piece of toast and your favorite juice for a hearty breakfast.

IDEA You can add diced onions, green peppers or even diced ham. Create your own version.

" This recipe is very special to me because my mother made this dish just for me when I was growing up. "

Cloud Nine Eggs

Nonnie's Kitchen
INGREDIENTS

6 Bread Slices
1-1/2 Cups Grated
    Cheddar or Monterrey
    Jack Cheese
1-1/2 Cup Half 'N Half
6 Extra Large Eggs
Salt
Pepper

prepare

Heat oven to 350 degrees. Arrange the slices of bread in a single layer in a shallow, greased 9x13-inch baking dish. Sprinkle the bread lightly with salt and pepper. Sprinkle the grated cheese evenly over the bread. In a separate bowl, slightly beat the eggs. Combine the eggs and milk and whip until blended. Pour the milk mixture over the bread and cheese. Cover the baking dish with plastic wrap and refrigerate for at least 6 hours.

bake

When you are ready to cook, bring the baking dish to room temperature. The bread will have absorbed all the liquid. Bake for 1 hour or until the bread is puffy and slightly brown on top.

serve

Serve with ham slices, fresh fruit and your favorite breakfast drink.

serves 4

Nonnie's Kitchen

INGREDIENTS

1 Box Cream of Wheat®
Butter
Maple Syrup
4 Tall Cylindrical Glasses

Fried Mush

prepare

Make 8 servings of the Cream of Wheat® by following the directions on the box. Pour equal amounts of prepared Cream of Wheat® into each of the four glasses. Cover with a paper towel and set on countertop overnight. The next morning, slide the "mush" out of the glasses and slice into 1/4 inch thick round pieces.

fry

Put a tablespoon of butter into a skillet. When the butter is sizzling it is time to put in some of the slices of mush. Brown on both sides. Continue cooking until all slices have been cooked and are brown.

serve

Serve on a breakfast plate with sausage, ham or bacon. All the mush needs is a little butter and a great maple syrup.

66 This breakfast dish is oh, so different and wonderfully delicious. Try with flavored syrup and berries on top . . . wow! 99

Are You Thirsty?

There are all kinds of beverages. The kind you drink with a meal, the kind you have with a snack, and those you enjoy as a dessert. Beverages are wet and usually pleasing to drink. They come in all kinds of flavors and all kinds of containers.

I have included some of my favorites that I know you'll love making and drinking. The nice thing about many of these recipes is that they are really easy to make and can be made one at a time.

Try them all and see if you can figure out which one is my favorite.

4 Sale Lemonade 10 Cents

Nonnie's Kitchen

INGREDIENTS

2 Cups Fresh Lemon Juice (about 14 lemons)
6 Squeezed Lemon Halves
2 Cups Water
3 Cups Sugar

prepare

In a large saucepan, cook the sugar with the water over medium heat, stirring until sugar is dissolved. Add 6 squeezed lemon halves. Bring to a boil. Reduce the heat and simmer uncovered for 5 minutes. Remove from the heat and cool. Stir in the fresh lemon juice. Cover and refrigerate until well chilled. Remove the squeezed lemon halves.

serve

Pour the juice in a pitcher and serve refreshingly.

66 This is about the best darn lemonade you'll ever taste . . . enjoy! 99

Lemonade Stand

Nonnie's Kitchen
MATERIALS

4 Milk Crates (or similar)
1 Large Cookie Sheet or Plywood
Bright Fabric or Colored Sheet
2 (5 Gallon) Buckets
Small Chalkboard
Coin Box or Piggy Bank

construct

Place 2 milk crates side by side then stack another on top of each crate. Place a large cookie sheet or a piece of plywood about 20x20 inches on top, forming a flat surface. Cover with bright fabric or a colored sheet. Use 5 gallon buckets upside down for seats.

decorate

Write on a small chalkboard or make your own signs. They can say something like, "Lemonade for Sale". Add your price for a glass and any other fun information about your refreshing lemonade. Don't forget the coin box so that you'll have somewhere to put the money from all of your sales.

IDEA Use your imagination and search around the house for other materials that might add to your lemonade stand. Be creative!

" You can draw or paint fun pictures on the colored sheet. It's certain to draw a lot of attention. "

Orange Grape Splash

Nonnie's Kitchen

INGREDIENTS

1 (12 oz.) Can Frozen Orange Juice Concentrate, Thawed
4-1/2 Cups Ginger Ale, Chilled
2 (25 oz.) Bottles Red or White Grape Juice
1 Pint Raspberry Sherbet
1 Orange, Sliced

prepare

In a punch bowl, gently stir together the orange juice and the ginger ale. Add the grape juice. Use a small ice cream scoop to scoop the sherbet into the punch bowl (see page 36). Arrange the orange slices on the top of the punch.

serve

Serve in clear glasses or themed party cups.

IDEA

Try slicing the top off of an orange, cutting edges in an up and down, zig-zag design. Clean out the inside of the orange and fill with your Orange Grape Splash. Freeze. After 2 hours or more, you will have a tasty splash-freeze . . . burrrrr!

serves 4

Fruitti Smoothie

Nonnie's Kitchen
INGREDIENTS

1 Cup Orange Juice
3 Cups Frozen Fruit Pieces
4 Teaspoons Sugar or
   Splenda®
1/2 Banana

blend

Put everything in a blender and pulse until all
ingredients are mixed together.

serve

Serve in tall colorful glasses. Decorate with
your favorite fruit slice, a colored straw and
a long handle spoon.

" Each kid will love to make their
own . . . and no wonder . . . this
smotthie is out of sight yummy . . . "

serves 2

Frozen Brown Cow

Nonnie's Kitchen

INGREDIENTS

3 Level Teaspoons Sweetened Cocoa
1-1/2 Tablespoons Sugar
1 Milk Chocolate Candy Bar (without nuts)
2 Cups Milk
Whipped Cream
Chocolate Sprinkles

cook

In a small sauce pan on low heat, cook the milk, sugar and cocoa. Mix well. Break up the candy bar and drop it in to the milk mixture and continue to mix until the candy bar has little pieces left in the pan. Cool for 15 minutes.

blend

In a quart-size blender, add crushed ice until half full. Add the chocolate mixture. Mix on high. The mixture should look like soft ice cream. If it is still liquid, add more crushed ice.

serve

Pour mixture into a large soda glass or a wide-mouth ice cream dish. Top with a mound of whipped cream and chocolate sprinkles. Insert two straws and an ice cream spoon.

"Sip and eat slowly because this drink is very cold, very tasty and mooing good."

Orange Icicle

Nonnie's Kitchen

INGREDIENTS

1 Cup Vanilla Ice Cream
1 Cup Orange Sherbet
2 Cups Orange Juice
2 Cups Crushed Ice

blend

In the following order, combine ice cream, sherbet, orange juice and ice in a blender so the ice doesn't get caught in the blender blade. Blend until thick and frosty.

serve

Garnish with an orange slice that you have poked a straw through.

IDEA

How about freezing in an icecube tray or popcicle mold? Insert popsicle sticks and freeze overnight for a refreshing treat.

> " Ice cream and orange sherbet go so well together and make a fantastic summertime snack. "

Chocolate Volcano

Nonnie's Kitchen

INGREDIENTS

2 Ounces Bittersweet Chocolate
1/2 Cup Chocolate Syrup
1 Egg
2/3 Cup Half N' Half
Chocolate Ice Cream
French Vanilla Ice Cream
Club Soda, Chilled
2 Tall Soda Glasses

prepare

Before you start gathering your ingredients, select 2 soda glasses. Rinse the glasses with cold water and place in the freezer.

microwave

Place the bittersweet chocolate in a microwaveable dish or a glass measuring cup. Melt the chocolate in the microwave on high for 1 minute. Add the chocolate syrup and mix well. Let the chocolate cool to room temperature.

blend

Place the chocolate syrup mixture, egg, half n" half, and 1 large scoop of chocolate ice cream in a blender. Blend for one minute.

serve

Divide the mixture between the 2 frosty glasses. Add about 2/3 cup of the club soda water to each glass. Drop 2 large scoops of vanilla ice cream into each glass. Top off the glasses with club soda water until the froth starts to spill over. Stick a crazy straw and a spoon into each glass and drink up.

Juice Fizz

Nonnie's Kitchen

INGREDIENTS

4 Cups Orange Juice

1-1/2 Cups Ginger Ale

1/4 Cup Maraschino
Cherry Juice

combine

Combine all of the ingredients.
Mix well and pour over ice.

serve

Top with a small paper umbrella, maraschino
cherry and a lime wedge or add a crazy straw.

IDEA No Ginger ale? Make your
own. Add a few drops of Coke®
to a glass of 7-UP®. Stir and taste.
Add more cola until it tastes like
Ginger ale.

> ❝ The fizz may tickle your
> nose, but the flavor is
> contagious... leaving you
> wanting more. ❞

Giraffe Float

Nonnie's Kitchen

INGREDIENTS

2 Scoops Vanilla Ice Cream
Cranberry Juice or
    Red Fruit Punch
1/4 Cup Miniature
    Marshmallows or
    Marshmallow Cream
1 Large Marshmallow
3 Maraschino Cherries
1 Plastic Straw

prepare

Run the straw through the center of the cherries and top with a large marshmallow. Set aside. Drop a scoop of vanilla ice cream into a tall glass. Pour enough cranberry juice or red punch into the glass to cover the ice cream. Drop the second scoop of vanilla ice cream into the glass and fill the glass with cranberry juice or red punch. Top with miniature marshmallows.

serve

Place the straw (the neck and head of the giraffe) and a long spoon into the glass.

" You are not going to want to share this one, but that's okay. Let your friends make their own with you. "

Junk Yard Soda

Nonnie's Kitchen
INGREDIENTS

1 Can Coca Cola®
1 Can 7-Up®
1 Can Dr. Pepper®
1 Can Root Beer
1 Can Oange Soda
1 Can Grape Soda

prepare

Be sure that your sodas are cold. Select a tall glass, rinse with water and freeze. Place 15 ice cubes in a large pitcher. Pour 2 cans of soda at a time into the pitcher. Once all of the cans have been poured, stir with a long-handled spoon.

serve

Remove frozen glasses and serve with 3 fun straws of your choice.

> " This is a real favorite for kids because they never seem to be able to make up their minds on which soda they want to drink... neither can I. "

Punch Ice Bowl

Nonnie's Kitchen
MATERIALS

2 Stackable Glass Bowls
Water
Licorice
Hard Candies
M&M's®
Wax Coke Bottles

construct

Fill the largest bowl half full with water. Insert next smaller size bowl into the water. Float the bowl so that you have approximately 1-1/2 inches of water thickness between them. Be sure that there is a 1 inch gap at the top of the large bowl so that the water can expand when it freezes. Place in freezer. Freeze until the water becomes thick and slushy, about 1 to 2 hours.

create

Remove the bowls from the freezer. Begin setting the licorice, candies and wax bottles into the slushy water. You'll know if you have the right consistency if the items stay where you place them in the water. If the items are floating, place the bowls back into the freezer until you have the right consistency. Continue placing your items between the bowls to create your own fun and unusual designs. Place the bowls back into the freezer for 24 hours.

serve

When ready to serve, remove the outer bowl and pour in your favorite beverage.

IDEA Instead of candies, come up with some edible goodies to create a special party theme for birthdays, holidays and just plain havin' fun.

Anytime Snacks

All kids love snacks. Did you know that snacks can be a good part of your daily nutritional requirements? It's true. These anytime snacks are both healthy and just plain yummy. You will enjoy these after school with your family or just about anytime.

A snack is usually enjoyed between breakfast and lunch and between lunch and dinner. However, I have included some snacks that are great anytime. Fruit, cookies, grains, gelatin, and Kluck Kluck Pretzel Chicken are among the fun snack ideas for you in this section.

Even though you are tempted, please don't substitute a snack for your regular meals.

Snack-A-Doodle

prepare

Put handfuls of your favorite ingredients from the list or add a few of your own favorite snack pieces to one of the plastic cups. (A handful for 3 - 5 year-olds, or 1 tablespoon for everyone else). When you have all the snack pieces in one of the cups, put the 2 cups rim-to-rim and shake. Shake 1-2-3 stop, shake 1-2-3 stop. You can even shake to your favorite music. Make sure all of the snack pieces end up in one of the cups. Remove the second cup and you have a ready-made snack.

Nonnie's Kitchen
INGREDIENTS

2 (8 oz.) Plastic Cups Per Person
Cheerio's®
Wheat Chex®
Rice Chex®
Raisins
Sunflower Seeds (shelled & unsalted)
Sliced Almonds
Granola
Dried Cherries
Banana Chips

66 This is a great travel treat for the entire family. So mix up a bunch and store in a sealed container. 99

Cracker Cookies

Nonnie's Kitchen
INGREDIENTS

8 Ritz® Crackers
4 Teaspoons Peanut Butter
3 Ounces White Chocolate

prepare

Spread the peanut butter on one side of a cracker. Cover with another cracker, making a sandwich.

microwave

Melt the white chocolate in the microwave for about 1 minute. With a set of tongs, dip each cookie in the melted white chocolate (Have a grownup help you with this because it will be hot). Place the cookie on a piece of waxed paper and let cool.

> " This is a recipe just for you. However, if you want to make a party out of this, double, triple or even quadruple this recipe and enjoy. "

Wiggly Fruit Gelatin

Nonnie's Kitchen
INGREDIENTS

1 Package Jello®
1 Cup Fruit Juice
2 Cups Fresh or Canned Fruit

prepare

Pour Jello® into a large bowl. Add 1 cup of boiling water. Mix well. Add 1 cup of your favorite clear fruit juice (pear, white grape juice, guava or lemonade). Mix until well blended. Set in refrigerator until chilled and a bit wiggly, about 45 minutes. Add 2 cups of fresh fruit pieces or well-drained canned fruit. You can choose from, bananas, strawberries, fresh raspberries, peaches, blueberries, or fruit cocktail. Do not use frozen fruit. Pour into your favorite mold. Put back into the refrigerator until very firm.

serve

Un-mold by setting the mold pan in a sink filled with warm water. Quickly remove the pan from the water. Hold a plate on the top of the pan and with 2 hands turn over quickly. Serve with dabs of whipped cream, or whipped topping.

IDEA
Use a crazy shape to go along with a party theme, such as flowers or cartoon characters.

Nonnie's Applesauce

Nonnie's Kitchen
INGREDIENTS

8 Granny Smith Apples
1 Cup Water
1/2 Cup Sugar
Cinnamon

prepare

Peel, core and quarter all of the apples.

cook

Put the water and apples into a saucepan. Bring the water to a boil then simmer until the apples are tender. Drain off all of the water. Mash up the apples with a potato masher or heavy-duty fork. Add the sugar to the apples and sprinkle with cinnamon. Blend well.

serve

Serve warm or cold in little bowls or dishes.

IDEA
Make a funny face with red-hots on a scoop of warm applesauce. Red-hots will eventually melt and make the applesauce pink.

66 Applesauce is a great snack by itself, or you can try it on toasted English muffins . . . really yummy. 99

A Chip Off the Olé Guacamole

Nonnie's Kitchen
INGREDIENTS

3 Ripe Avocados
2 Tablespoons Fresh
   Lemon Juice
1/4 Cup Diced Tomatoes
1/4 Cup Water Chestnuts,
   Diced
1 Teaspoon Garlic Salt
1 Teaspoon Pepper
Tortilla Chips

prepare

Peel the skin off of the avocados. Put avocados in a bowl and mash with a fork. Add the lemon juice, diced tomatoes, diced water chestnuts, garlic salt and pepper. Mix well and enjoy. Note: Depending on the firmness of the avocados more lemon juice may be needed.

serve

Serve in a bowl surrounded by your favorite tortilla chips, celery or carrot sticks. This is a great anytime snack.

Yellow Dogs in their Blanket

Nonnie's Kitchen
INGREDIENTS

1 Package Ready-Bake Biscuits or Croissants
24 Little Hot Dogs or Sausage Dogs
1 Cup Shredded Cheddar Cheese
Mustard

microwave

Put the little hot dogs in a microwavable dish. Cover with the water. Cook in the Microwave on high for 2 minutes. Let Cool.

prepare

Heat oven to 450 degrees. Cut biscuit triangles into 2 pieces making smaller triangles. Spread a thin layer of your favorite mustard on each piece. Place one little dog at the large end of the dough and sprinkle with a teaspoon of cheese. Roll the dog up in its blanket. Place the doggies on a cookie sheet.

bake

Bake for 15 minutes or until golden brown.

serve

For a fun idea, serve in that back of a toy fire truck or dump truck. This is sure to get your friends barking.

Purple Roll-Ups

serves 4

Nonnie's Kitchen
INGREDIENTS

4 Thin Flour Tortillas
1/2 Cup Grape Jelly
1 Cup Whipped Cream Cheese

prepare

Use cream cheese and jelly that is at room temperature. Mix together the jelly and the cream cheese. Spread about 1/4 of the mixture over each tortilla. Be sure your mixture goes all over the tortilla. Roll each of the tortillas up starting at the side closest to you. Roll the tortilla very tightly. Wrap each rolled tortilla individually in plastic wrap and refrigerate for 1 hour.

serve

Cut the tortilla into 8 to 10 slices about 1-inch thick. Serve with a glass of milk.

66 You can do what I do
and eat the whole roll,
but be carefull . . . this is
a messy one. 99

2 Bread Slices
2 Ice Cream Scoops of
Peanut Butter
1 Tablespoon Sweet
Pickle Relish
1/2 Banana, Sliced

Gooey Peanut Butter Goodies

prepare

Place your bread on a plate. Drop a scoop of peanut butter on each slice of bread and spread with a knife. Add the banana slices to one slice of bread, and the sweet pickle relish to the other slice. Put the two slices together and cut in halves.

serve

Serve with a big glass of cold milk and some potato chips.

IDEA
You can use a large cookie cutter and cut out fun shapes, depending on the occasion.

"Try this . . . you'll like it. It sounds a little funny, but Nonnie says YUM."

Cereal Pops

Nonnie's Kitchen
INGREDIENTS

5 Cups Rice Crispies®
3 Cups White Raisins
1/4 Cup Margarine
1 (10 oz.) Bag Small
   Marshmallows
1/3 Cup Powdered Kool-Aid®
12 (7 oz.) Plastic Cups
12 Lollipop Sticks

prepare

In a large bowl combine the cereal and raisins. Set the bowl aside.

cook

In a medium saucepan, melt the margarine. Add the marshmallows. Cook over low heat, stirring continuously until the marshmallows are thoroughly melted and the mixture is smooth. Stir in the Kool-Aid® drink powder. Pour the mixture evenly over the cereal and raisins. Mix well. Spray the inside of the cups with vegetable spray. Spray your fingers with vegetable spray as well so the mixture does not stick to your little fingers. Pack the mixture into the cups. Fill each cup 3/4 full and push in a wooden stick all of the way to the bottom. Cool completely.

serve

To remove the pops from the cups turn the cups upside down and tap.

IDEA
When having a themed party or for a special occasion, use different designs, patterns or your favorite cartoon character cups. Place one at each place-setting as a take home party favor. Don't be surprised if it doesn't make it home

Nuttie Apples

Nonnie's Kitchen
INGREDIENTS

1 Medium Apple
2 Tablespoons Peanut Butter
1/4 Cup Pecans, Chopped
1/4 Cup Raisins

prepare

Core the apple and cut into 8 wedges. Spread your favorite peanut butter evenly over one side of the apple wedge. Dip each wedge into chopped pecans and raisins.

serve

You can serve on a plate or just simply eat as you go.

> **"** My mother always told me that apples would make me grow up healthy and were sure to make me wise. No matter what kind of apple you choose, I think that my mother's advice will work for you, too. **"**

Trash

prepare

Heat oven to 200 degrees. Combine all ingredients except butter, salt and Worcestershire, in a very deep bowl.

cook

Melt the butter in a saucepan and add the seasoned salt and Worcestershire sauce. Pour over the dry mixture and mix well.

bake

Pour mixture into a deep baking pan. Bake for 2 hours turning the mixture every 15 minutes.

serve

Let cool and enjoy.

Nonnie's Kitchen
INGREDIENTS

2 Cups Corn Chex®
2 Cups Rice Chex®
2 Cups Cheerio's®
4 Cups Pecans
2 Cups Pretzels
  (round or sticks)
2 Cups Melba Toast, Broken
2 Sticks Butter
1/4 Cup Seasoned Salt
3/4 Cup Worcestershire
  Sauce

" Don't be surprised if your friends want the recipe and the instructions to make their own. I'll bet you never thought that you'd be eating a snack out of a trash bag. Don't worry . . . I won't tell anyone. "

Trash Bag

1 Large Brown Grocery Bag
Paraffin (this can be found in the canning section of the grocery store)
1 Large Stockpot or Washtub.
Tongs

cook

A grownup needs to supervise this entire activity. Using the large stockpot or washtub, melt 1 box of paraffin over medium heat.
Cook only until all of the paraffin is dissolved. Paraffin needs to be melted but not boiling hot.

construct

Roll the grocery bag from the top down as if rolling up your jeans. When half of the bag is rolled, you can begin the dipping process. Lay numerous sheets of newspaper or butcher paper on a flat counter. With the tongs, begin dipping the bag. Do not submerge bag totally in the paraffin because there will be no place to hold on to the bag. Paraffin can be very hot. The paraffin will cool very quickly once it is on the bag so keep dipping until you have the bag completely covered in paraffin. Set the bag down on the newspaper pour a ladle full of paraffin into the bottom of the bag and spread around. Mold the bag to the shape you desire. Go crazy when shaping the bag.
Tie colorful ribbon or raffia around the bag. Place a paper towel in the bottom of the bag and fill with Trash or your favorite treats.

IDEA You can make smaller containers from smaller brown bags. Insert a small bowl inside the bag. Decorate for any occasion and serve bread, vegetables, potatoes and anything else you can imagine.

Rockin' Salsa

INGREDIENTS

1 (32 oz.) Can Diced Tomatoes
2 Teaspoon Fresh Cilantro
1 Teaspoon Fresh Limejuice
1/2 Onion, Finely Chopped
2 Tablespoons Salad Oil
1 Diced Green Pepper

prepare

Dice tomatoes, green pepper and onions. Tear or cut cilantro into small pieces. Add lime juice and salad oil and toss all ingredients.

serve

Serve in a decorative southwestern bowl with chips. Spoon over eggs or serve on your hamburger, chicken - even hot dogs.

66 Salsa is used more as a condiment, than Ketchup. Can you believe that? 99

Southwest Dippin' Sauce

1 Lb. Ground Sausage

1 (12 oz.) Can Evaporated Milk

1 Lb. Soft Cheddar Cheese

4 Tablespoons Salsa

(recipe on previous page)

fry

In a large skillet, brown and break up the sausage until fully cooked. Remove the sausage from the pan and place on paper towels to soak up the excess grease. Replace the sausage in the pan and add all of the other ingredients. Heat until the cheese is melted and the mixture is hot.

serve

Pour into a warming dish or Mexican clay bowl. Serve with corn chips.

66 Even though you will be tempted, keep fingers out of the sauce, but enjoy to the last drop. 99

Kluck Kluck Pretzel Chicken

Nonnie's Kitchen
INGREDIENTS

2 Lbs. Skinless, Boneless
Chicken Breasts
1/2 Cup Prepared Mustard
2 Cups Crushed Pretzels

prepare

Heat oven to 400 degrees. Cut the chicken into 2-inch strips. Pour mustard into a shallow bowl. Using a brush, coat the chicken strips with the mustard on both sides. Roll the coated chicken in the crushed pretzels. Place the chicken on a baking sheet that has been sprayed with vegetable oil.

bake

Bake for 5 to 8 minutes or until chicken is browned and fully cooked.

serve

Serve on a platter with extra mustard for dipping and frilly-ended or themed-ended toothpicks.

> " These little chicken bites are like popcorn . . . you pop them in your mouth and can't stop eating them. "

Little People Popcorn Balls

Nonnie's Kitchen
INGREDIENTS

1/4 Cup Margarine
1 (10.5 oz.) Bag Miniature Marshmallows
1/2 Cup Powdered Drink Mix or Flavored Gelatin
12 Cups Popped Popcorn
Raisins
Almonds
Cherries

microwave

Combine margarine and marshmallows in a large microwave safe bowl. Microwave for 2 minutes or until marshmallows are fluffed up. Stir in powdered mix until well blended.

combine

Pour the marshmallow mixture evenly over the popped popcorn in a large mixing bowl. Stir until the popcorn is well coated. Let cool a bit. Have a grownup spray your hands with vegetable spray. Shape the popcorn mixture into balls. Place on waxed paper for decorating.

decorate

Before they cool, decorate the Little People using raisins as eyes, almonds for the nose and slices of cherries to make the mouth.

IDEA

You can use rope licorice and M&M's® to make hair and other parts of the little people's faces. Create puppets or unique center-pieces using popcorn balls for the head and styrofoam for the body.

Snake Skin Cheese

Nonnie's Kitchen
INGREDIENTS

1 (12 oz.) Softened
   Cheese Spread
10 Ritz® Crackers
10 Saltine Crackers
2 Raisins
Cracker of Your Choice

prepare

Place 20 crackers in a plastic, closable bag. With your hands, smash the crackers into little pieces. Set aside. Tape down a piece of waxed paper on the counter. Be sure the surface is flat. Using your hands, scoop out the cheese spread and place it on the waxed paper. Roll out the cheese using the palms of your hands to create a snake-like shape. Pour the crackers onto the waxed paper. Roll the cheese into the crackers and completely cover. Place the raisins on the end as eyes.

serve

Place your cheese snake on a platter for all to see. Serve with a cheese knife surrounded by more yummy crackers.

> " Grownups often tell you not to play with your food, but this is one time when I am sure that they will make an exception. "

Good Stuff

Healthy food can be yummy. Not all of the foods that you say you don't like taste the same – it depends on how they are prepared. In this section I have created some good-tasting and good-for-you recipes that I know you'll want to cook with family and friends. The best part is... you get to eat them, too.

These recipes make great side dishes or small meals. Pair them with your favorite breakfast or dinner recipes and enjoy. Remember, good stuff is good for you and yummy too.

Baked Potato Head

INGREDIENTS

1 Baking Potato Per Person
Vegetable Oil
Butter
Sour Cream
Shredded Cheese
Chives
Peas

prepare

Choose a medium to large potato. Scrub the potato with a vegetable brush (not your tooth brush). Rub the potato with oil. Poke the skin of the potato 3 times with a fork. Grownups will appreciate this because it will keep the potato from exploding. Wrap fully with plastic wrap.

microwave

Cook the potatoes in the microwave for 4 minutes per potato (cook 2 potatoes for 8 minutes). Be careful when removing the hot potato from the microwave. Let cool 2 minutes before unwrapping the potato.

serve

Cut the potato down the center. Fluff the inside of the potato with a fork. Add the toppings you like best. Believe it or not, my favorite is ketchup. You can experiment with anything that you like, too.

IDEA

When serving, make potato heads. Use vegetables such as broccoli for hair, carrots for arms and peas for the eyes.

Squishy Squash

Nonnie's Kitchen

INGREDIENTS

1 Acorn Squash
4 Teaspoons Butter
1/4 Cup Maple or
   Berry Syrup
4 Tablespoons Chopped Nuts

prepare

Heat oven to 400 degrees. Have a grownup slice the squash in half. Place the squash on a baking sheet or in a round pie pan. Poke the inside of the squash with a fork several times. Put 2 teaspoons of butter on each half of the squash. Pour the syrup over both halves. Sprinkle 2 tablespoons of chopped nuts over each half.

bake

Bake until squash is soft and tender, approximately 1 hour. Scoop out the squash from the skin and serve.

> **"** This is a dish that you really must try. Like mashed potatoes, squash can be creamy and delicious. **"**

Kernel Kob

serves 4

Nonnie's Kitchen
INGREDIENTS

4 Ears Corn on Cob
1 Stick Butter
Salt
Pepper

microwave

Place buttered corn in a microwaveable dish. Sprinkle with the salt and pepper. Cover with plastic wrap. Be sure the plastic wrap forms a seal over the corn. Cook in the microwave for 20 minutes (about 5 minutes for each ear of corn). When removing the corn from the microwave, let a grownup help because the dish will be very hot. Let the corn cool for 5 minutes and then remove the plastic wrap. Open the side furthest from you just to let the steam escape.

" This is a great side dish to your favorite hamburger or grilled meat. This can be your contribution to a great dinner. Corn is so fun to eat! "

Fruit Granola Parfait

Nonnie's Kitchen
INGREDIENTS

1 (8 oz.) Flavored Yogurt
1/2 Cup Granola Mix
1 Sliced Banana
1/2 Cup of your favorite Berries
1 Very Tall Glass

prepare

Pour half of the yogurt in the bottom of the glass. Add half of the granola and half of the fruit. Pour the rest of the yogurt on top. Top with the rest of the granola, sliced banana and fruit.

> " You will need a long spoon to eat this and mix up the goodies as you go. This is a healthy, nutritious and filling snack or side dish for breakfast. It's super yummy. "

INGREDIENTS

6 Canned Pear Halves,
   Drained
1 (6 oz.) Package Soft
   Cream Cheese
2 Tablespoons Crushed
   Walnuts
6 Lettuce Leaves
Salad Dressing

Pear Salad

prepare

Mix cream cheese and nuts together. Spoon a tablespoon of the mixture into the center of each pear.

serve

Place a piece of lettuce on a small oval plate and set the prepared pear on top. Serve with your choice of dressing. French or Catalina dressings taste great. You can also use pecans or other nuts.

" This was my favorite salad when I was a child. I used to wait to see who wasn't going to eat theirs, so that I could have more. I know you'll enjoy this, too. "

Rice N' Round Broccoli

Nonnie's Kitchen
INGREDIENTS

1 Cup Cooked Rice
1 (12 oz.) Package Frozen
   Broccoli Florets
1 (8 oz.) Jar Cheese Whiz®
1/2 Cup Celery, Chopped
1 Regular Can Cream of
   Mushroom Soup
1 Regular Can Cream of
   Chicken Soup
1 Teaspoon Paprika

prepare

Heat oven to 350 degrees. Make rice according to package directions or use left-over rice. Grease a round casserole dish. In a mixing bowl, add all of the ingredients to the cooked rice, except the paprika. Do not add water or liquid to soups. Pour the rice mixture into the greased baking dish. Sprinkle with paprika.

bake

Bake for 30 to 40 minutes or until golden brown on top.

" Even if broccoli isn't your
favorite vegetable, I promise
. . . you'll love this recipe. "

Humpty Dumpty Eggs

Nonnie's Kitchen

INGREDIENTS

6 Hard-Boiled Eggs
2 Drops Hot Sauce
   (not big drops)
1 Tablespoon Sweet Pickle
   Relish
Mayonnaise
Celery Salt
Paprika

boil

Hard-boil the eggs in a small saucepan by carefully putting eggs into the pan. Gently cover with water and cook on high. Let boil for 10 minutes. Let the eggs cool before you continue. Peel the shell off of the eggs.

prepare

Slice each egg in half lengthwise. Using a teaspoon, scoop out the yellow yolk centers. Mash the yolks with a fork. Add the sweet relish and hot sauce and mix completely. Add the mayonnaise a teaspoon at a time and mix to a firm, but creamy consistency. Very carefully spoon the egg mixture back into each egg half. Chill until ready to serve.

serve

Place the eggs on a round plate or platter. Form a circle around the plate with the eggs. Make another circle inside the first circle and continue until the last egg ends in the middle. Sprinkle with paprika.

Din Din

Dinner for me, while growing up, was a time for the entire family to come together and share a wonderful meal and the busy day's events.

The meals were balanced and included dishes like meatloaf, potatoes, a green vegetable, salad and. . . a dessert - if we had been good that day.

Life has changed a lot over the years and dinnertime can be rushed and hectic, trying to get out of the house for Scouts, music lessons or soccer games. So I have created quick, nutritious and tasty nightly meals that can be eaten and prepared in a timely manner.

Dinnertime is still a good time to talk to your parents about the things that are happening in your life, the problems that need fixing and planning for the next family outing.

Enjoy preparing and eating these fun and delicious recipes on the pages that follow. I know these will become some of your favorites.

Family Kabob

Nonnie's Kitchen

INGREDIENTS

- 1 Lb. Sirloin Beef or Steak
- 1 Onion
- 2 Large Tomatoes
- 12 Small New Potatoes
- Barbeque Sauce
- Italian Dressing

prepare

Cube the uncooked beef. You can use shrimp or cubed chicken as well. Quarter the tomatoes and the onion. Use wooden or stainless steel skewers to build your Kabobs by alternating the meat, tomato, onion and potato until you fill your skewers. Brush the kabobs with barbeque sauce or Italian dressing.

grill

Have a grownup cook on the grill, until the meat is thoroughly cooked and the vegetables are browned.

serve

Serve one kabob per person. Serve with a salad for a yummy outdoor meal.

IDEA

The younger children can put each item for the kabobs on the skewers and the older children can prepare the meat and vegetables for the grownups to grill.

Lavosh for kids

Nonnie's Kitchen
INGREDIENTS

1 Large Lavosh (or several small 8-inch lavosh)
1-1/2 Cups Diced Muenster Cheese
1 (8 oz.) Package Pepperoni Slices
1 Cup Diced Tomatoes
1/2 Cup Sliced Raw Mushrooms
1 Cup Canned Corn, Drained
1 Cup Cooked Broccoli Florets
1/2 Cup Cooked Peas
1/2 Cup Diced Cooked Chicken
1-1/2 Cups Diced Havarti Cheese

prepare

Heat oven to 375 degrees. Place the Muenster cheese on the large lavosh or on the individual lavosh. Add your favorite ingredients from the selection of toppings. Lastly, top the lavosh with the Havarti cheese.

bake

Bake until cheese bubbles, about 10 to 15 minutes.

serve

Cut the large lavosh into "pizza slices".

IDEA Other ingredients you might like to try can include: olives, hearts of palm, artichoke hearts, onions or even pine nuts. Be creative! Add some of your own favorites as well. Great to serve at parties.

Quesadilly Guacadilla Olé

INGREDIENTS

2 Flour Tortillas
1/2 Cup Jack Cheese, Shredded
1/8 Cup Guacamole
   (see recipe page 42)
1/4 Cup Sour Cream
1 Cup Diced Cooked Chicken
Salsa
   (see recipe on page 50)

IDEA Make many for your family and friends and have a fiesta!

prepare

Put one tortilla on a microwaveable dish. Spread with guacamole, then with the sour cream. Spread diced chicken evenly over the tortilla. Sprinkle the cheese over the entire tortilla. Add some of your favorite salsa. Top with the other tortilla and cover with a damp paper towel.

microwave

Microwave on high for 1 minute.

serve

Cut into 4 pieces. You can add more sour cream or salsa on top if you like.

Kernel Chick Soup

cook

Heat the milk and butter in a suacepan until warm and butter is melted. Add salt, pepper and sugar into the pan. Stir and continue heating. Add the can of drained whole-kernel corn. Add the can of cream corn. Add your meat or shrimp and heat to a slight boil, stirring frequently.

Nonnie's Kitchen
INGREDIENTS

1 (15 oz.) Can Whole Kernel Corn
1 (15 oz.) Can Cream Corn
2 Cups Milk
1 Tablespoon Butter
1/2 Teaspoon Salt
1/2 Teaspoon Pepper
1 Teaspoon Sugar
2 Cups Sausage, Chicken or Shrimp, Prepared
Sour Cream

serve

Ladle into a soup cup and top with a dab of sour cream. Serve with your favorite buttery crackers or cheddar cheese.

> " This is a recipe that I love to make and enjoy on a cold evening when I can get all cozy in the kitchen and cook with my grandchildren. "

Nonnie Max's Meatloaf

Nonnie's Kitchen
INGREDIENTS

2 Lbs. Ground Chuck
1 Extra Large Egg
1/2 Cup Italian Bread Crumbs
1 Cup Ketchup
1-1/2 Tablespoons Onion Salt
1 Teaspoon Pepper

prepare

Heat oven to 375 degrees. In a large bowl mix together the meat and the egg. Add the breadcrumbs, half of the ketchup, onion salt and pepper. Here comes the fun. Wash your hands well with soap and water. Pick up half of the mixture in your hands and form into a ball. Do the same with the rest of the mixture. Combine the two halves of the meat with your hands and form into a loaf-like shape. Place the meatloaf in a 9x13-inch baking dish. Pour the rest of the ketchup over the meat and spread with your hands.

bake

Pop the meatloaf into the oven for about 45 minutes or until nice and brown on top. Have a grownup remove the meatloaf from the oven. Let cool for 5 minutes.

serve

Slice into 1-inch pieces and serve. You may serve this with applesauce, a baked potato and a green vegetable for the perfect family meal.

Moon Burger

prepare

With a fork, break up the meat. Tear the cheese into quarter-size pieces. Toss the meat and the cheese together lightly, pressing them into a round shape. Make 4 patties from the mixture.

grill

Have a grownup cook the burgers on the grill or broil the patties in the oven. Lightly toast the English muffins. Place the patties on the English muffins and dress with your favorite condiments.

Nonnie's Kitchen
INGREDIENTS

1 Lb. Ground Chuck
1/4 Lb. Swiss Cheese
4 English Muffins
Tomato
Lettuce
Ketchup
Mustard
Relish
Mayonnaise

IDEA For a *Blue Moon Burger* substitute Blue Cheese for the Swiss. For a *Cheesy Moon Burger* substitute cheddar cheese.

Dandy Lasagna

prepare

Heat oven to 375 degrees. Pour half of the sauce in an un-greased 9x13-inch pan. Add half of the water and mix together. Place 1/3 of the ravioli over the sauce. Cheese, meat or spinach ravioli will work great. You can use frozen, but defrost the ravioli first. Sprinkle 1 cup of the grated mozzarella, 1/3 cup grated romano or parmesan cheese. Make a second layer of ravioli, mozzarella and romano or parmesan cheese. Continue with a third layer of the same. Mix the rest of the water and sauce together and pour over the dish.

Nonnie's Kitchen
INGREDIENTS

- 1 (26 oz.) Jar Marinara Sauce
- 1 Cup Water
- 1 (20 oz.) Package Fresh Ravioli
- 3 Cups Grated Mozzarella Cheese
- 1 Cup Grated Romano or Parmesan Cheese

bake

Cover with foil and bake for 1 hour. Uncover and sprinkle with the rest of the cheese. Bake 10 minutes more. Remove from the oven and let stand for 5 minutes.

serve

Scoop up and enjoy. Serve with a slice of your favorite bread and a salad.

Chili Rellenos

INGREDIENTS

2 (7 oz.) Cans Green Chilies
1 Cup Sharp Cheddar Cheese, Shredded
1/2 Cup Whole Milk
1/2 Teaspoon Dry Mustard
4 Large Eggs
1/2 Teaspoon Salt

prepare

Heat oven to 350 degrees. Butter a 9x13-inch baking dish. Open the cans of chilies and rinse under cold water until water is clear. Pat the chilies dry with a paper towel. Layer half of the green chilies in the bottom of the baking dish and sprinkle with half of the cheese. Make another layer with the green chilies and cheese. In a separate bowl, beat the eggs and add the milk, salt and mustard. Pour this mixture over the layered chilies and cheese.

bake

Bake for about 35 minutes or until bubbly on top. Let cool 5 minutes.

serve

Cut into 8 squares and serve. Be sure to scoop out the bottom layer of chilies. This is a great dish for the whole family and so good with a Caesar salad.

Cheese Fun-nini

INGREDIENTS

4 White Bread Slices
4 Slices American Cheese
8 Teaspoons Yellow Mustard
4 Tablespoons Butter
Tomatoes (optional)

prepare

Preheat a waffle iron that has been sprayed with vegetable oil. Spread 1 teaspoon of the mustard on one side of each slice of bread. Place a square of cheese on each slice of bread. If you love tomatoes, now is the time to add a slice before grilling. Put the two sides together and butter the outside of the sandwich.

cook

Place your sandwich carefully in the preheated waffle iron. Close the top as firmly as you can. It is okay if the top doesn't close all of the way. Let it cook for 3 minutes.

serve

Serve with chips, a pickle and a glass of milk. This is about the best and most fun cheese sandwich you will ever have.

Chicken Drumettes

Nonnie's Kitchen

INGREDIENTS

8 Chicken Legs
1/4 Cup Grated Parmesan Cheese
1-1/2 Cups Seasoned
    Breadcrumbs
1/2 Cup Vegetable Oil

prepare

Heat oven to 350 degrees. Wash chicken legs in cold water until water runs clear. Wrap the end of each leg with foil. When the legs are cooked you can hold the leg by the foil tip. In a bowl, mix the breadcrumbs and cheese together. Pour the vegetable oil in a wide-mouth bowl. Cover each leg with oil and dip into breadcrumb mixture, covering the entire leg. Avoid oiling or breading the foil tip. Place on a foil lined cookie sheet.

bake

Bake for 35 minutes or until chicken is crisp and golden brown.

serve

Serve with rice and a salad for a great family meal.

> " Cook this recipe the day before
> you go on a picnic or road trip.
> Keep cool and enjoy. "

Triple Decker Mac N' Cheese

INGREDIENTS

1 (24 oz.) Package Large Elbow Macaroni
4 Cups Sharp Cheddar Cheese, Shredded
24 Saltine Crackers
6 Tablespoons Butter
1/3 Cup Milk
Pepper

prepare

Boil macaroni until cooked, but not soft. Drain and slightly cool. Do not rinse. Place crackers in a plastic, closable bag and lightly crush into pea-size or larger pieces. Set aside. In a 9-inch round casserole dish, place 1/3 of the macaroni. Take 2 tablespoons of butter and cut into 8 to 9 pieces and lay evenly over the macaroni. Sprinkle with pepper to taste. Cover with 1/3 of the cheese. Repeat 2 more layers to end with 3 layers of macaroni, butter, pepper and cheese. Pack as firmly as you like so that all of the layers fit well in the casserole dish leaving space for the cracker topping. Top with the crushed crackers. Now for the fun part. Using your index finger, slip it down along the edge of the inside of the casserole dish, making a slight hole. Pour 1 tablespoon of the milk into the hole. Repeat along the edge of the dish 3 more times.

bake

Bake at 375 degrees for 45 minutes or until golden brown on top.

serve

Let cool for 5 minutes and scoop onto a plate. Serve with peas and a salad for the best macaroni and cheese you'll ever have.

Zerts

When you're hungry, isn't it funny that the first thing you think of to eat is dessert? Well you are not alone, because dessert represents pleasing and delicious thoughts for us all. In fact, I often find myself planning dinner around dessert. There are so many choices, from cold, refreshing ice creams, to soft velvety pies and creamy cheese cakes.

Desserts are usually served after a meal or on a special occasion. You may not have dessert every night, but when you do, it is usually a special treat. Desserts can be healthy or just plain indulgent. They can be salty, sweet or bitter, but no matter what the taste - everybody loves a great "zert."

I know you are going to love the desserts that you will prepare from the recipes on the pages that follow. I know that each recipe will represent a happy time in your life and a memory you'll want to share.

Chocolate Macaroons

INGREDIENTS

- 1 (14 oz.) Can Condensed Milk (fat free, sweetened)
- 1 (14 oz.) Package Shredded Coconut
- 1 Teaspoon Vanilla
- 1 Lb. Chocolate, White or Dark

prepare

Heat oven to 350 degrees. Line a cookie sheet with parchment paper or a silicone baking sheet. Mix the condensed milk, coconut and vanilla in a bowl until well blended. Drop by teaspoons full onto the cookie sheet.

bake

Bake for 10 to 12 minutes. Let th cookies cool on the cookie sheet.

cook

Melt the chocolate in a double boiler or put in a microwavable bowl and cook on high for about 1 minute. Dip half of the cookie in the chocolate and place on waxed paper to dry. The chocolate will be very hot, so have a grownup help you.

serve

These macaroons are incredible with or without the chocolate and take no time to make.

IDEA

Try some macaroons in a bowl with fresh strawberries and a dab of whipped cream on top for a great tasting dessert.

Chocolate Tamales

Nonnie's Kitchen
INGREDIENTS

1 (16 oz.) Package White Chocolate
(for best results use chocolate specifically made for candy making)
1 (4 oz.) Package Chopped Pecans
1 (4 oz.) Package Chopped Walnuts
Tamale Cornhusks
Raffia Ties

cook

Melt chocolate in a double boiler or in the microwave for 1 minute. Chocolate will be very hot. Mix until creamy and fully melted. Add the pecans and walnuts until blended.

prepare

Separate husks until you have approximately 20 individual husks about 4x6 inches in size. Spread a small amount of the melted chocolate mixture on the inside center of the husks. Fold the left side over the chocolate and then the right side over the left. Tie a piece of natural-colored raffia around each chocolate tamale to hold shape. Let the chocolate tamales cool.

serve

This makes for a great dessert for the whole family or a small party. Once the tamale is opened, the chocolate is like a small chocolate bar and a fun treat.

White Coconut S'mores

makes 4

Nonnie's Kitchen
INGREDIENTS

8 Graham Crackers
4 Large Marshmallows
16 Squares White Chocolate
4 Teaspoons Shredded
   Coconut

prepare

Place a 4-square piece of chocolate on each of 4 graham crackers.

toast

Bend a coat-hanger into a long skewer and place a marshmallow on the tip. Toast until it is golden brown over an open flame with a grownup's supervision. This is a great thing to do while camping or in the backyard over the grill.

serve

Place the toasted marshmallow on top of the chocolate. Sprinkle with coconut and top with another graham cracker.

SAFETY TIP You want to stay as far away as you can from the fire. A grownup must be present to assist you in toasting the marshmallows. Never try this by yourself.

Pineapple Yum

Nonnie's Kitchen

INGREDIENTS

8 Bread Slices
1 (20 oz.) Can Crushed
   Pineapple
1 Egg
1 Cup Sugar
6 Teaspoons Butter

repare

eat oven to 350 degrees.
ease a 9-inch baking dish.

ombine

osely mix all of the ingredients in a large bowl.
ur mixture into the baking dish.

ake

ave a grownup put the dish into the oven and bake for approximately 1
ur or until the top is crisp and golden brown. Cool slightly
d serve.

> "Enjoy as a snack or you can
> even eat with dinner as a side
> dish. For a great dessert, top
> with ice cream ... yummy!"

Ah-so Rice Pudding

Nonnie's Kitchen
INGREDIENTS

2 Cups Cooked Rice
1 Cup Sugar
1 Cup Milk
1 Teaspoon Vanilla
4 Large Eggs
2 Tablespoons Butter
1 Teaspoon Cinnamon

prepare

Heat oven to 250 degrees. In a bowl, mix the eggs until well blended. Add the milk and vanilla and mix well. Add the sugar. Put the rice in a small casserole dish making sure to break up any large pieces of rice. Be sure the rice is at room temperature. Pour the milk mixture over the rice. Drop the butter in the middle of the rice mixture. With the back of a mixing spoon, spread the butter over all of the rice. Place cinnamon in the palm of your hand and sprinkle over the rice mixture.

bake

Bake in the oven for 35 to 40 minutes.

serve

Scoop out and serve warm or refrigerate for a great sweet and cool dessert.

IDEA Add a half cup of raisins or a half cup of blueberries to the rice mixture before baking for more great flavors.

Southwest Pillows

Nonnie's Kitchen
INGREDIENTS

4 Cups Sifted Flour
1 Tablespoon Baking Powder
1 Teaspoon Salt
3 Tablespoons Shortening
Vegetable Oil
Water
Powdered Sugar

prepare

n a Bowl, combine the flour,
aking powder and the salt.
lend in the shortening. Add enough water to make the dough soft.
oll out the dough to 1/4-inch thickness. Cut into 3-inch squares.

ake

ave a grownup help you to prepare for frying. Deep fry the
quares in hot oil until golden brown. Remove with tongs and drain
n paper towels. Dust with powdered sugar.

serve

erve with honey, flavored syrup or jelly.

> " They are so delicious and
> comforting that you will want to
> make enough to share
> with everyone. "

Chocolate Krunch Bites

Nonnie's Kitchen
INGREDIENTS

2 (6 oz.) Milk Chocolate
   Candy Bars
2 Cups Cheerio's®
2 Cups Kix® Cereal

microwave

Put the chocolate in a microwaveable dish,
and melt in the microwave for 1 minute. Cool slightly.

combine

Fold in both cereals until well coated with the chocolate. Drop
the mixture by tablespoons full onto waxed paper. Place the
Chocolate Kluck Bites in the refrigerator until set.

serve

These are so good you won't worry about how to serve them.
But, they make a great small dessert after dinner or you can
put them in a baggy and save some for later.

66 The great thing about these is
that there is a different flavor
in every crunch. You won't be
able to hide and eat these. 99

Thank Goodness for Pralines

makes 12

Nonnie's Kitchen
INGREDIENTS

1 (16 oz.) Box Brown Sugar
1 Cup Whipping Cream
3 Cups Chopped Pecans

prepare

Mix the brown sugar and the cream together. Pour the mixture into a saucepan and cook over medium heat until mixture starts to thicken, about 3 minutes. Stir in the pecans and cook 3 minutes more. Drop by teaspoon onto waxed paper and let cool.

serve

Place on a plate for all to eat.

IDEA

Make the perfect gift by taking colored plastic-wrap and cut into 6-inch squares. Wrap the candies, twist and tie with your favorite ribbon.
This makes a fun "anytime" gift.

Nuttie Blueberry Yogurt Pie

Nonnie's Kitchen
INGREDIENTS

2 (8 oz.) Containers Blueberry
  Yogurt
1 Cup Whole Fresh Blueberries
1 (8 oz.) Container Whipped
  Topping
1 Cup Chopped Pecans
1 Ready-Made Graham
  Cracker Crust

prepare

In a bowl, combine yogurt and half a cup of the blueberries. Fold in the whipped topping. Spread the chopped pecans over the bottom of the ready-made pie crust. With your finger tips, level the nuts on top of the crust forming a nutty layer. Pour the yogurt and blueberry mixture into the pie crust and spread evenly. Put the pie into the freezer for at least 4 hours.

serve

Remove from the freezer 30 minutes before serving. Slice the pie in 8 serving pieces and top each slice with the remaining blueberries.

" Blueberries have never had it so good.
Cool, creamy and delicious . . . perfect
for a hot summer's day. "

Toasted Almond on a Stick

Nonnie's Kitchen
INGREDIENTS

1/2 Gallon French Vanilla Ice Cream
1-1/2 Cups Sugar-Coated Cereal Flakes
1/4 Cup Toasted Almonds, Chopped
10 Popsicle Sticks

prepare

Use a medium size ice cream scoop to form an ice cream ball. Be sure the ice cream isn't too soft, but soft enough to scoop into a ball. Clean your hands well. Take the ice cream ball out of the scoop and roll it in a mixture of the cereal flakes and almonds. Be sure to cover the entire ice cream ball. Set ice cream balls in a glass dish and insert an ice cream stick in the top of each. Be sure that the ice cream treats are not touching. Freeze for 2 hours or more, covered with clear plastic wrap.

serve

Take out as many ice cream treats as you need and cover the remaining ice cream balls with clear plastic wrap saving them for later.

Child-Proof Cheesecakes

Nonnie's Kitchen
INGREDIENTS

1-1/2 Cups Graham Cracker Crumbs (about 10 graham crackers)
1-1/2 Cups Butter, Melted
3 Tablespoons Sugar
3 (8 oz.) Packages Cream Cheese, Softened
3/4 Cup Sugar
1 Teaspoon Vanilla
3 Extra Large Eggs
3 or 4 Colored Decorating Gels
Colored Sprinkles

prepare

Heat oven to 350 degrees. Put the graham crackers into a closable plastic bag. Take a rolling pin and roll over the crackers until they are completely broken into crumbs. You can use chocolate or original graham crackers for the crust. Put the graham cracker crumbs into a mixing bowl and add 3 tablespoons sugar and the melted butter. Mix well with a fork. Pour the crumbs into a 9x13-inch baking pan and push the crumbs evenly over the entire bottom of the pan. Using an electric mixer on medium speed, mix the cream cheese, vanilla and remaining sugar. Add the eggs and continue mixing until there are no lumps in the mixture and it appears to look like cream. Pour the cream cheese mixture over the crust.

bake

Bake for 30 minutes or until the center is almost set.
Cool for 30 minutes and refrigerate overnight.

serve

When you are ready to serve, cut the cheesecake
into 12 squares. Serve on a dessert plate with a
doily under the piece of square cheesecake.

IDEA Get your decorating gel tubes or
pens and sprinkles. Write your family
or friend's name on their square. Draw
flowers or make a fancy looking gift
box. Use your imagination and see how
incredible they will look.

" How do you know the center
is set? Put a toothpick in the
middle of the cheesecake and
pull it out. If the toothpick
comes out clean, it's done. "

Crispy Apple Crunch

Nonnie's Kitchen
INGREDIENTS

4 Cups Sliced Granny Smith
  Apples
1/4 Cup Sugar
2 Tablespoons Water
1-1/2 Cups Bisquick®
1/2 Cup Sugar
1/4 Cup Butter, Melted
1 Tablespoon Cinnamon
1 Egg
1 Pint Vanilla Ice Cream

prepare

Heat oven to 350 degrees. Grease a 9-inch baking dish. Peel and slice the apples. Arrange the apples in the bottom of the baking dish. Sprinkle the apples with the water. Sprinkle the apples with 1/4 cup sugar. In a bowl, mix the Bisquick®, 1/2 cup of sugar and the cinnamon. In another bowl slightly beat the eggs. Pour the eggs over the dry mixture and stir with a fork into pea-sized crumbs. Pour the crumbled mixture evenly over the apples. Melt the butter and pour over the entire dish.

bake

Bake for 25 minutes or until golden brown on top.

serve

Serve warm with ice cream.

IDEA

You can use your favorite fruit, such as peaches or cherries in place of the apples. Be sure to drain well if using juicy fruits.

Holidays

Holidays are exciting times of the year. Everyone gets in a great mood as they prepare for the grand festivities. As a child, I always went overboard with ideas, making invitations, placemats, streamers, front door signs, favors and - oh yes - dressing in theme for every holiday.

I had the best time and still do. Every holiday is important, but I have selected a few for us to go overboard with . . . together. You and your family and friends will enjoy preparing these special treats together. Please don't forget the decorations, have fun and happy holidays to all.

Celebrate

Birthdays

People of all ages love having a birthday party. Just get creative. Decide on your theme, gear up your imagination and start preparation for the best parties yet.

IDEA For invitations, why not take a picture of the birthday boy or girl and place it on a colorful piece of construction paper. Use colored crayons to write out the information about the party. Change colors every few letters or every other word.

ANOTHER IDEA For a swimming party, tie a "message-in-a-bottle" from your favorite inflatable pool toy and give them out as invitations. Add a note about the details of the party, roll up the deflated toy and mail it to your friends - and wait for the "wave" reviews.

MORE IDEAS Make a DVD or CD about the birthday boy or girl and the fun-things planned for their party. Or, how about a puppet party. Invitations go on decorated paper bags that have the details for the party written on them. Include instructions telling your friends to bring the bag filled with materials to make their own puppets.

serves 8

Birthday Celebration Pie

prepare

In a large bowl, spoon the softened ice cream. You can use strawberry, chocolate or your favorite, but remember you have lots of sweets going on, so try to stay simple with your choices. Crush the graham crackers and the 7 chocolate bars in 1/4-inch pieces. Gently fold in the graham crackers, chocolate bars, almonds and the sliced banana. Spoon the mixture into the graham cracker crust. Smooth the top of the pie with the back of a spoon. For the topping, garnish the top with the M&M's®, chocolate bars, almonds and marshmallows. Freeze until firm, about 2 hours.

serve

When you serve, you can decorate with plastic cartoon characters, with candles or curly ribbon - resulting in plenty of giggles and fun.

Nonnie's Kitchen
INGREDIENTS

7 Bite-Size Hershey's® Chocolate Candy Bars (Chunky and Plain)
1 Banana, Sliced
1 Quart Vanilla Ice Cream, Softened
9 Whole Chocolate Graham Crackers
1/2 Cup Almonds, Chopped
1/2 Cup Miniature Marshmallows (colored or white)
1 Ready-Made Graham Cracker Crust (chocolate or regular)

Topping
7 Bite-Size Hershey's® Chocolate Candy Bars, Broken
2 Tablespoons Unblanched Almonds, Chopped
1/2 Cup M&M's® Candy
1/2 Cup Miniature Marshmallows

Easter

With springtime, Easter is celebrated bringing family and friends together. Parades, Easter bonnets and colorful dress can be as much a part of Easter as a great meal. I have included some of my favorite Easter recipes and ideas that I know your family will enjoy and share together.

IDEA How about doing a fun-themed Easter egg hunt. Get some colorful plastic eggs and fill them with wrapped candy and a message from you. Think about what your family and friends mean to you and let them know.

ANOTHER IDEA Fill a jar or large glass container with jelly beans, counting each yellow jelly bean as you place it in the jar. On Easter, ask everyone to guess the correct number of yellow jelly beans. Whomever comes closest to your number with out going over, wins a special prize that you can create.

Hippity Hop Bunny Cake

prepare

Heat oven to 350 degrees. Grease and flour two 9-inch cake pans. In a large bowl, use an electric mixer to blend the cake mix, pudding, oil, eggs, water and grape juice. After ingredients are blended, mix on high for 3 minutes. Pour cake mixture evenly into cake pans.

bake

Bake at 350 degrees for 30 minutes or until a toothpick comes out clean. The cake needs to be cooled completely before cutting. Cut cake as shown in diagram creating the bunny ears and the bow tie.

Nonnie's Kitchen
INGREDIENTS

1 Box White Cake Mix
1 Small Box Instant Vanilla Pudding
1 Cup Vegetable Oil
4 Extra Large Eggs
3/4 Cup Cold Water
1/2 Cup White Grape Juice
1 (16 oz.) Container Vanilla Frosting
6 Cups Shredded Coconut
Green and Red Food Coloring
3/4 Cup Chocolate Chips
Red String Licorice
2 Large Jelly Beans
1 Large Gum Drop

decorate

Put frosting on all sides of the cake pieces. Assemble pieces as shown in diagram on a cookie sheet, flat basket or a tray covered with aluminum foil. You can use colored foil. Frost the top of the cake. Sprinkle about 2-1/2 cups of the coconut evenly over the top and sides of the entire cake. With your hands, press the coconut to sides of the cake. In a bowl, tint about 3/4 of a cup of coconut with 2 to 3 drops of red food coloring. Toss with a fork until evenly colored. The coconut should be pink. In another bowl, use the rest of the coconut and add 4 drops of green food coloring and toss with a fork until all the coconut is green. Sprinkle the pink coconut in the center of the bunny ears and bowtie, leaving a white outline of 1 inch. Outline the bowtie and ears with chocolate chips Decorate your bunny face using jellybeans for the eyes, a gumdrop for the nose and llcurice for the whiskers and mouth. Sprinkle the green coconut around the perimeter of the Bunny Cake to look like it is lying on grass.

serve

Use Mr. Hippity Hop Bunny as your Easter center-piece and then enjoy.

diagram

Easter Stained Glass Fruit Salad

Nonnie's Kitchen
INGREDIENTS

- 2-1/2 (16 oz.) Cans Fruit Cocktail, Drained
- 2 (16 oz.) Cans Pineapple Chunks or Tidbits, Drained
- 1 Small Bottle Marachino Cherries, Drained
- 1/2 Cup Chopped Pecans
- 1/2 Cup Miniature Marshmallows
- 1/2 Pint Whipping Cream
- 1 (3 oz.) Package Cream Cheese, Room Temperature
- 1/2 Cup Miracle Whip®

prepare

In a large bowl, soften cream cheese. Be sure it is at room temperature. Blend cream cheese and Miracle Whip® together. Mix well. Add all of the other ingredients except the whipping cream. Whip the cream to soft peaks and fold into the mixture. Pour mixture into a quart-size milk carton that has been cleaned and dried, leaving the top open and the bottom of the carton closed. Note: You can use 2-quart size milk cartons or a half-gallon size carton. Hold the top of the carton together with a large paper clip or a binder clip. Freeze for 2 days.

serve

When ready to serve, cut the milk carton and peel it away from the frozen salad. Cut the fruit salad into serving sizes.

" This salad will dazzle you with an array of color and satisfy your every tastebud. "

Fourth of July

The Fourth of July signals the middle of summer. It's a sparkling day, full of fun, laughter and colorful fireworks. Picnics and swim parties are bountiful with stars and stripes flying high. This is a day when family and friends come together and celebrate our independence.

The Fourth is usually a very hot day . . . and what a great day for ice cream.

IDEA Call family and friends together for a Fourth of July celebration wearing the colors of the day – red, white and blue. Make it fun and use your imagination. Everyone will see that you are in the spirit of the day.

ANOTHER IDEA Construct top hats for each of your friends using red, white and blue construction paper. Form the hat making a cylinder of blue, rim of red and white stars all over.

Homemade Ice Cream

Nonnie's Kitchen
INGREDIENTS

Electric or Manual (hand turn)
   Ice Cream Maker
3-1/4 Cups Sugar
3 Tablespoons Flour
10 Extra Large Eggs
1-1/2 Teaspoons Salt
12 Teaspoons Vanilla
1-1/2 Teaspoons Lemon Extract
5 Pints Whipping Cream
5 Cups Rock Salt
1/2 Gallon Whole Milk
3 (5 Lb.) Bags Ice
Dish Towel

prepare

Freeze the ice cream maker's metal can and paddle for up to 1 hour before using. Put the eggs in a large mixing bowl and mix with an electric mixer until foamy. Continue mixing while adding the flour, sugar, salt, vanilla and lemon extract. Slowly add in the whipping cream.
When finished adding the cream, stop mixing. Fill each of the empty pint-size whipping cream containers with milk. Note: Do not use 1%, 2%, or Skim Milk. ONLY use Whole Milk. Swish milk around and pour into the mixture. With a large wooden spoon, blend in the milk. Pour immediately into the chilled metal can and fill with more milk up to 2 inches from the top. Give a taste. If you need a little more vanilla for your taste, add a teaspoon at a time. Put in the paddle and snap on the top. Lift the metal can into the large bucket, lining up the grooves in the bucket and container. Place the motor or crank mechanism on top of the bucket and fasten. Fill with approximately half a bag of ice and sprinkle with 1 cup of rock salt. Continue layering ice and salt until filled to the top of the ice cream cylinder.

Place a towel over the ice, being careful not to cover the motor. Plug in the ice cream machine to begin the churn. If you are using a hand-crank, begin churning. Note: It may be necessary to add more ice and salt as you churn to ensure the ice and salt layers remain at the top of the cylinder. When the machine slows or stops, the ice cream is ready. With a crank, when it becomes too hard to churn, the ice cream is ready. Take the motor or crank off of the cylinder. Completely wipe off the salt from the top of the metal container before opening the lid. The ice cream will be creamy, but you're going to have a hard time keeping everyone from wanting a taste. After tasting, pour the ice cream into freezer containers and freeze about 5 hours as a final step.

serve

Serve in your favorite bowls and top with fresh berries, syrups or enjoy just the way it is. Be careful not to eat the ice cream too quickly – it's very cold!

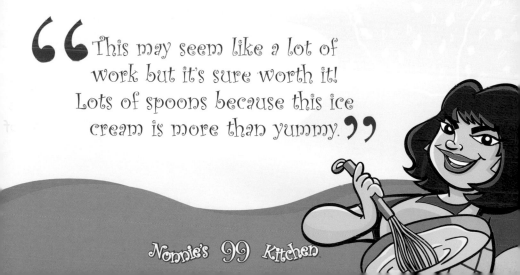

" This may seem like a lot of
work but it's sure worth it!
Lots of spoons because this ice
cream is more than yummy. "

Halloween

Fall, for me, was a great time of year because I got to see the seasons begin to change. Watching the leaves turn brilliant colors of yellow, orange and red always put me in the spirit of Halloween.

Every Halloween I had many ideas about what I wanted to be, so no one ever knew what to expect. The neighbors always had special treats and the decorations were fun but scary. I love to add a little fun and fright in the kitchen, and what better time than Halloween to make Creepy Hands and Dirt Pot Cake. But remember to be careful, for you never know what might be lurking around the corner.

IDEA Make it fun and easy for your friends to "trick or treat" at your house. How about carving many smaller pumpkins with funny faces, placing candles inside and setting them along the walk way to your front door?

ANOTHER IDEA Make all of your decorations using only orange and black crepe paper. Some fun ideas can include dressing up the front door to look like a pumpkin. Cover the whole door with orange and then create black shapes for the eyes and mouth and tape them on the door. Or, you could hang the crepe paper above the door, making a jungle of black and orange fringe for "trick or treaters" to pass through before they ring your doorbell.

Halloween Creepy Hands

Nonnie's Kitchen
INGREDIENTS

12 Cups Microwave Buttered
Popcorn
4 Plastic or Rubber
Preparation Gloves
20 Pieces Candy Corn
4 Colored Rubber Bands
4 Spider Rings
4 Ribbon Pieces,
6 Inches Long

prepare

Open each plastic glove and drop a candy corn into each finger of the glove. Fill with popcorn making sure each candy corn stays in place to look like finger nails. When the glove is filled up to 1 inch from the top, twist and close with a rubber band. Tie a colored bow around the rubber band and hang.

IDEA

You can use creepy hands as a party favor or as a place setting. For real fun, when the "trick or treaters" come to your door, stick out a creepy hand and you'll have a lot of howling going on.

ANOTHER IDEA

Fill a set of plastic gloves with water and tie-off the end. Freeze overnight. At party time, remove the glove and put the hand of ice into a punch bowl. For Fun, put a plastic spider ring on one of the fingers and watch everyone scream.

Dirt Pot Cake

construct

Paint a wacky scary face on each of the pots. Once dry, line all the pots with colored foil leaving the foil hanging over the pot. Cut the overhang foil in small strips to resemble hair. You can even curl it by rolling it up with a pencil.

prepare

Nonnie's Kitchen
INGREDIENTS

- 1-1/4 Pounds Chocolate Cookie
- 1/2 Cup Butter or Margarine
- 1 (8 oz.) Package Cream Cheese, Softened
- 1 Cup Powdered Sugar
- 1 (12 oz.) Container Whipped Topping
- 1 (6 oz.) Package Instant Vanilla Pudding
- 8 Flat-Bottom Ice Cream Cones
- 8 (2-inch) Terracotta Flowerpots
- 1 Package Gummy Worms
- 1 Package Gummy Flowers
- Colored Foil

Crush the cookies in a closable plastic bag and seal the bag. Take a rolling pin and roll over the cookies to roughly crush. Sprinkle half of the cookie crumbs evenly in the bottom of each cake cone. Pat the crumbs into all of the corners. Beat together the butter and the cream cheese using an electric mixer. Add the sugar and beat until creamy. Fold in the whipped topping. Using half of the mixture, spoon an equal amount over the crumbs in the bottom of each cone. Prepare the instant pudding according to the directions on the package. When the pudding is thickened, spoon half of the pudding into each cone. Finish with the rest of the whipped topping and pudding, making another layer. Top with the remaining cookie crumbs. Decorate the tops with wiggly gummy worms and a few gummy flowers.

serve

Set each of the 2-inch terracotta pots on a saucer. Set a cone in each pot and serve with a spooky spoon.

Hanukkah

Hanukkah, a celebration of light, is a wonderful holiday reserved for children and children-at-heart. On each of 8 nights, a candle is lighted to start the celebration. Dreidle are spinning and songs are sung while each child receives a gift to open.

The food is symbolic and latkes and candle salad are two of the dishes that are greatly anticipated for what's to come.

IDEA Make your own Hanukah gelt. Take chocolate candy wafers and wrap with gold colored foil. Use these "coins" or gelt and give to the winner of the Dreidle game.

Hanukkah Candle Salad

Nonnie's Kitchen
INGREDIENTS

2 Bananas
4 Sliced Rings Canned Pineapple
4 Orange Gumdrops
Lettuce
Mayonnaise
1 Kiwi

prepare

Cut the bananas in half and remove the tips. Put a dollop of mayonnaise in the center of each of the pineapple rings and place on a small plate. Stand a banana in the center of each pineapple ring to represent the candle. With a toothpick, place a gumdrop on top of each banana to represent the flame. Cut off the ends of the kiwi and cut it in 4 equal slices. Make a small slit on the outer edge of each pineapple base. Wedge the kiwi in the slit standing up the kiwi slice, to form a handle for your candle. You can spread a little mayonnaise on the side of the banana to represent melted wax.

serve

Set each place-setting with a candle salad to represent the celebration of light.

Latkes Spud Pancakes

Nonnie's Kitchen
INGREDIENTS

6 Medium Potatoes
1/2 Onion
? Extra Large Eggs
1/2 Cup Flour
1 Teaspoon Salt
Vegetable Oil

prepare

Peel the potatoes. Grate the potatoes and the onion in a mixing bowl. Add the eggs, flour and salt. Stir until all the ingredients are blended. You may need a little more flour if the mixture is too wet, in order to keep pancakes together.

fry

Pour about 1 inch of oil in frying pan. Heat the oil until it crackles when droplets of water touch the oil. Drop the batter from a tablespoon into the oil, making 3 to 4 per batch. Flatten with the back of a spoon, making 2-inch pancakes. Fry over medium-high heat, until brown on underside, then turn and brown the other side. Lift out with a spatula and place on a paper towel to drain. Continue method until all batter is gone.

serve

Serve with applesauce (see recipe on page 41), jelly and sour cream. Or you can just eat them plain.

TIP

If you have leftovers, and I doubt you will, place 2 pancakes in a paper towel. Wrap and place in a plastic closable bag. Latkes will keep for up to 1 month. To reheat, remove frozen latkes and place in the microwave for about 1 minute, Check to make sure they are warm. Remove paper towel and serve.

Christmas

Christmas is a grand holiday filled with wonderful dreams, cherished memories and imagination for all. A time for children to rejoice in the merriment of the season, celebrating the meaning of Christmas while waiting for Santa to slide down the chimney, bearing gifts of toys only dreamed about until now.

Holiday preparation starts early, days before what will be an elaborate feast. An edible gingerbread house, Mr. Snowman and cookies that glisten like stars all abound in the next few pages. Oh what fun it is for one and all . . .

Mr. Snowman Cheese Ball

INGREDIENTS

4 (8 oz.) Packages Cream
   Cheese, Softened
1 Stick Butter, Softened
1 Teaspoon Minced Onion
2 Teaspoons Dried Dill Weed
2 Teaspoons Dried Chives
2 Teaspoons Dried Parsley
2 Teaspoons Lemon Pepper
2 Raisins
7 Dried Cranberries or
   Dried Cherries
1 Large Round Cracker, 3-inch
2 Chocolate Oreos®
2 Carrot Sticks
1/4 Cup Coconut
Cracker Assortment

prepare

Cream the butter and 3 packages of the cream cheese together with a wooden spoon. Combine the onion, dill weed, chives, parsley and pepper together. Add to the cream cheese mixture. Blend Well. Chill covered for 2 hours. Form into two balls. One ball should be smaller than the other for the snowman's head. Coat cream cheese on the outside of both cheese balls. Be sure to leave 2 tablespoons of cream cheese for use later. Place small cheese ball on top of larger cheese ball. Touch up in places that you need to with cream cheese. Place two raisins for the eyes, one cranberry for the nose and four cranberries across for the mouth. Place the large round cracker on the head, as the rim of the hat. Place a small amount of cream cheese on the center of the cracker and place an Oreo® cookie on top. With a dab of cream cheese, place a second Oreo®, making the entire hat. Sprinkle the coconut around the plate for decoration.

serve

Serve on a bright colored plate with various crackers or toasted bite-size breads such as bagel chips.

Nonnie's Kitchen
INGREDIENTS

1 Pound Butter, Softened
1 Cup White Sugar
1 Large Egg
1/4 Teaspoon Salt
1 Teaspoon Baking Powder
4-1/2 Cups Flour
1 Cup Flour
1-1/2 Teaspoon Vanilla
1 (16 oz.) Container White
  Frosting
Food Coloring

Spritz Cookies

prepare

Heat oven to 375 degrees. In a large mixing bowl, add butter and sugar. With an electric mixer on medium, mix the sugar and butter together. When the sugar and butter are mixed, turn the mixer to low and add your egg, salt and baking powder. Mix well. Add the vanilla and slowly add the flour. Mix until all of the ingredients look like one (not very long - maybe 1 minute). Use the extra cup of flour to dust a cookie mat or a wooden cutting board. Flour your hands and a rolling pin well. Take the dough out of the bowl and form it into a ball. Divide it into 6 pieces. Put one piece of the dough at a time on the cookie mat and roll out to a 1/2-inch thick piece. Use various Christmas cookie cutters and cut out the cookies.

bake

Place the cookies on a cookie sheet and bake for 10 to 12 minutes, or until lightly brown. Take cookies out of the oven and set on a plate to cool, before you decorate.

ecorate

Frost the cookies with red & green frosting. To make colored frosting, separate the amount of white frosting you'll need for each color. Put a few drops of food coloring in the frosting. Note: May be stored in an airtight container for up to 1 month.

IDEA

Use a tree-shaped cookie cutter to make a Christmas tree cookie. Frost with green frosting. Add different colors of frosting on the branch-ends to look like Christmas ornaments. For different holidays, all you have to do is change the cookie cutter and frosting colors. Be creative.

"You will need lots of help, but what a fun way to spend a Saturday afternoon making these delicious and festive cookies with a very special grownup."

Yule Time Gingerbread Cottage

construct base

Begin by wrapping your colored foil around the cardboard, forming a platform for where your cottage will be built. Take each of three whole graham crackers and pipe a thick line of icing on the right outside edge of the cracker. Place these 3 graham crackers together to make one side-panel of the cottage. Put together the other 3 graham crackers the same way completing the sides of the cottage.

Now build your back and front panels, each with 2 graham crackers. Pipe the inside edge of 2 crackers and place together to create the front-panel. Repeat for the back-panel.

Spread a thicker layer of frosting on the bottom edge of one side-panel and place on your foil platform. Hold in place for 60 seconds until the icing hardens. Now pipe the edge of your front wall on the bottom and right edges. Place at 90 degree angle and set. Repeat with the other outside wall-panels. Let the frosting completely dry before you continue.

MATERIALS

18 Graham Crackers
2 Graham Cracker Quarters
2 Ice Cream Sugar Cones
1 Package Miniature
  Marshmallows, Colored
1 Package Brach's Wreath
  and Tree Candies
1 Large Bag Whole Almonds
6 Ready-Made Frosting
  Tubes, White
2 Batches Gingerbread Icing
  (see recipe on page 112)
26 Candy Canes
Miniature Sled & Reindeer
1 (16-inch) Round Piece of
  Cardboard
Colored Foil

construct roof

Use 4 graham crackers to complete each side roof-panel. Heavily frost the right edge of 1 graham cracker place side-by-side with another. Continue until 4 graham crackers make up the roof panel. Repeat this step for the other side of the roof. Let the frosting completely dry before you continue.

On the top edge of each roof panel, pipe the frosting very thickly and join the two halves together on a 45 degree angle forming the rooftop. Let the frosting completely dry before you continue.

Place the roof on the house and observe where the frosting needs to go in order to secure the roof. Spread on the frosting to set the roof. The roof should hang over approximately 1/2 to 1 inch on all sides of the house. Let the frosting completely dry before you continue, this may be overnight.

There will be triangle gaps at the front and back of the house. Use a quarter piece, or larger, of your graham cracker to fill in these gaps. Don't worry if the frosting is thick everywhere, because when you decorate your cottage all will be covered. Let the frosting completely dry before you continue.

decorate

Make a Christmas tree for the front of the house. Mix 1/2 cup frosting and 3 drops of green food coloring. Cover the sugar cones with a thick layer of green icing. Decorate with sprinkles. To set in place, ice the bottom of the cones and hold firmly on the foil until set. Spread a thin layer of icing on the remaining platform area. Randomly place the marshmallows to create a snow drift effect. Dot the edges of the roof with the decorating tube frosting all around the house, which will drip to form icicles.   (continue, next page)

(continued)

To complete the roof, frost one side of each almond and put in place until roof is covered. Use the candy canes to form a fence around the cottage by frosting the bottom and the crook of the cane and putting together on a slant, one-by-one. Construct your window and front doors by piping with white tube frosting and add colored candies, as you like. Put the wreath on the door, Santa and his reindeer on the roof, and you have your very own cottage for the holidays.

Gingerbread Cottage Icing

prepare

Nonnie's Kitchen

INGREDIENTS

2 Lbs. Powdered Sugar
6 Tablespoons Meringue
    Powder (you can buy this
    at a cake decorating store)
1/2 Cup plus 2 Tablespoons
    Hot Water

Before you begin, rinse beaters and bowl in 2 tablespoons of vinegar per quart of water solution. Dry thoroughly. Put all of the ingredients in a glass or metal bowl only. This will keep your icing from falling. Mix together at high speed, when using a hand mixer; or medium speed when using a freestanding mixer. Mix until blended and thick in consistency. Note: Only make one batch at a time. You will likely need 2 batches.

The Glossary

This glossary of terms will help you to better your knowledge of cooking. These are just some of the important words and definitions that you will encounter throughout this book. Knowing what these terms mean, will make any recipe go more smoothly and it will ensure great results.

Glossary

BAKE: To cook by dry heat in an oven.

BEAT: To mix well with a fork, whisk or electric beater. Remember to look at your recipe to find out which cooking tool to use.

BLEND: To combine ingredients together.

BOIL: To heat a liquid until it has lots of bubbles, roaring at a fast pace.

BREAK UP: To make your item smaller, piece-by-piece.

BROWN: To cook very quickly, darkening on both sides.

BRUSH: To spread a liquid, like a barbeque sauce or glaze on food, usually using a pastry brush.

CHOP: To cut food into small pieces using a knife or food chopper.

COMBINE: To add ingredients together in a specific order.

CREAM: To whip until the consistency is smooth and well blended.

CUT IN: To take butter or a shortening and cut it up to blend with flour. You can use 2 knives, 2 forks or a pastry cutter to do this.

CORE: To take out the center or core of a vegetable or fruit.

CUBE: To cut food into small square-like pieces, about 1/4 inch to 1/2 inch.

Glossary

DAB: A spoon-sized amount of something, like butter or whipped cream, that is put on top of a dessert before it is put in the oven or served.

DEEP FRY: To cook food in deep oil so that it is completely covered.

DICE: To cut food into tiny cubes about 1/8 inch.

DOLLOP: A small amount, such as a teaspoonful, to garnish a dish.

DOT: To drop butter in small bits over food to be cooked

DRAIN: To pour off liquid from food by pouring through a strainer.

DUST: To sprinkle food lightly with spices, sugar or flour for a light coating.

FOLD: Gently bringing a rubber spatula down through the mixture, across the bottom and up over the top, gently blending.

FRY: To cook food in hot oil over medium to high heat.

GRATE: To take a large piece of food, like cheese, and rub it against a grater to make fine threads.

GRILL: To cook food on a grill over an open flame.

GREASE: To use a vegetable shortening spray or to spread butter with a paper towel over the bottom and sides of a baking dish. When making a cake, you may need to flour.

Glossary

KNEAD: To mix and work dough into a smooth elastic consistency. This can be done by hand or machine.

MARINATE: To soak food in a seasoned liquid mixture for a certain length of time.

MASH: To crush a food into a smooth and evenly textured state.

MELT: To heat slowly until it becomes liquid.

MINCE: To cut food into very tiny pieces. Minced food is smaller than diced food.

MIX: To add several ingredients together to make a recipe.

PACK: To press firmly into a measuring cup or dish.

PEEL: To remove the rind or skin from a fruit or vegetable using a knife or vegetable peeler.

PREHEAT: To warm an empty oven or appliance to the specified temperature.

QUARTER: To divide into 4 pieces.

SEASON: To add flavor to foods with salt, pepper, hot sauce or various spices.

SHRED: To cut food into thin strips. You may use a grater.

Glossary

SIFT: To put through a flour sifter or a fine strainer, eliminating lumps and bumps in flour.

SIMMER: To cook food in liquid over medium heat so that it does not boil.

SKIN: To remove the skin from food before or after cooking.

SLICE: To cut into 1/4-inch to 1/2-inch portions.

SPOON: To take mixed ingredients and put into a pan or dish, spoon-by-spoon.

SPRINKLE: To lightly and equally cover foods with an ingredient.

STEAM: To cook food on a rack or in a steamer basket over boiling water in a covered pan.

STIR: To mix or blend thoroughly.

SOFTEN: To bring butter, lard or vegetable shortening to room temperature.

TOSS: To mix ingredients loosely together.

WHIP: To beat ingredients until light and fluffy. This will add air to the ingredient.

Measurements

A Pinch	....	1/8 Teaspoon or less
3	Teaspoons	1 Tablespoon
4	Tablespoons	1/4 Cup
8	Tablespoons	1/2 Cup
12	Tablespoons	3/4 Cup
16	Tablespoons	1 Cup
2	Cups	1 Pint
4	Cups	1 Quart
4	Quarts	1 Gallon
16	Ounces (Oz.)	1 Pound (Lb.)
32	Ounces	1 Quart
1	Ounce	2 Tablespoons
8	Ounces	1 Cup

NOTE

Nonnie asks that you use standard measuring
spoons and cups and be sure that all measurements
are level.

Nonnie's Kitchen: Fun and Food in the Kitchen with Kids
COOKBOOK ORDER FORM

ATTN: BOOK ORDERS
M2M Partners Publishing
7825 E. Redfield Road, Suite 101
Scottsdale, AZ 85260

❏ Check if gift.

Please send me _____ copies at $16.95 per copy plus $6.95 per copy for shipping and handling. Orders for multiple copies contact us at: orders@nonnieskitchen.com
Enclosed is my check or money order for_____ .   (AZ residents add 7.95% for state sales tax.)

Name:_____

Address: _____

City: _____ Sate:_____ _____Zip:_____

Phone:_____

❏ Payment Enclosed   Charge My: ❏ Visa   ❏ MC   ❏ AMEX

Card Number: _____ _____ Exp. Date: _____

Signature: _____

Billing Address if different from above:

Address: _____ _____

City: _____ Sate:_____ Zip:_____

U.S. Funds & U.S. Delivery only. Contact publisher for bulk orders & foreign delivery at orders@nonnieskitchen.com.
Make checks payable to: M2M Partners Publishing
Ask us about our other products at orders@nonnieskitchen.com

- ✂ -

Nonnie's Kitchen: Fun and Food in the Kitchen with Kids
COOKBOOK ORDER FORM

ATTN: BOOK ORDERS
M2M Partners Publishing
7825 E. Redfield Road, Suite 101
Scottsdale, AZ 85260

❏ Check if gift.

Please send me _____ copies at $16.95 per copy plus $6.95 per copy for shipping and handling. Orders for multiple copies contact us at: orders@nonnieskitchen.com
Enclosed is my check or money order for_____.   (AZ residents add 7.95% for state sales tax.)

Name:__ _____

Address: _____

City: _____ Sate: _____ Zip:_____

Phone:_____

❏ Payment Enclosed   Charge My: ❏ Visa   ❏ MC   ❏ AMEX

Card Number: _____ Exp. Date: _____

Signature: _____

Billing Address if different from above:

Address: _____

City: _____ Sate:_____ Zip:_____

U.S. Funds & U.S. Delivery only. Contact publisher for bulk orders & foreign delivery at orders@nonnieskitchen.com.
Make checks payable to: M2M Partners Publishing
Ask us about our other products at orders@nonnieskitchen.com

Notes

Watar c every mo*

PBORG8G5V

or
2**

Notes

Notes

_____

_____

_____

_____

_____

_____

_____

_____

_____

_____

_____

_____

_____

Notes

Notes

Notes

Notes

My hope is that you enjoyed learning your way around the kitchen and have had many opportunities to cook with and for your friends and family. This book is just a beginning into the wonderful world of cooking with Nonnie. As you grow, so will your cooking abilities. And Nonnie will provide more recipes and more fun in the series of books to follow.

Good Cooking,

With Love,

Nonnie